ARTIFICIAL INTELLIGENCE

COLLECTION

PROMPT ENGINEERING

Volume 1

FUNDAMENTALS

STRUCTURING CONCEPTS

HISTORY OF PROMPT ENGINEERING

Prof. Marcão – Marcus Vinícius Pinto

Disclaimer:

Please note that the information contained in this document is for educational and entertainment purposes only. Every effort has been made to provide complete, accurate, up-to-date, and reliable information. No warranty of any kind is express or implied.

By reading this text, the reader agrees that under no circumstances are the authors liable for any losses, direct or indirect, incurred as a result of the use of the information contained in this book, including, but not limited to, errors, omissions, or inaccuracies.

ISBN: 9798343477368

Publishing imprint: Independently published

Summary

Welcome!

Artificial intelligence (AI) has proven to be a transformative force in multiple fields, from automation to the analysis of large volumes of data.

In the midst of this advancement, prompt engineering emerges as one of the central elements for harnessing the potential of generative AI models.

The book Prompt Engineering – Volume 1: Fundamentals, Structuring Concepts, History of Prompt Engineering is the first step to explore this fascinating discipline, bringing the reader the necessary foundations to understand and apply this new form of interaction with intelligent systems.

This volume is part of the "Artificial Intelligence: The Power of Data" collection, a series designed to deepen the understanding of fundamental AI concepts.

Available on Amazon, the collection provides a learning journey for those who want to master the languages and tools that move this digital age, revealing data as the essence of information and information as the essence of knowledge.

In prompt engineering, this value chain manifests itself explicitly: by structuring the interactions between humans and machines, the prompt becomes the key to unlocking the full potential of artificial intelligence.

Aimed at technology professionals, developers, data scientists, and AI enthusiasts, this book serves as a clear and in-depth introduction to the topic.

If you work with AI or want to start your journey in this field, this volume is essential to understand how well-crafted prompts can maximize the efficiency of models and algorithms.

In addition, managers looking to optimize the application of AI in their business will also find value here, as correct prompt engineering can be decisive in extracting more accurate and personalized results from their technological solutions.

The work brings a solid approach to:

- What is prompt engineering

- Core elements of an effective prompt

- Benefits and Objectives of Prompt Engineering

- Requirements to Become a Successful Prompt Engineer

- Risks associated with incorrect prompts

- History of the evolution of AI prompts, including techniques such as Transformers and LSTMs

- Applications and practical scenarios of prompt engineering

To make it easier to understand, the book includes real-world examples that demonstrate the application of prompt engineering in developing meaningful human-AI interactions.

For example, we'll look at how a poorly crafted prompt can lead to ambiguous or harmful results, while a well-structured prompt can personalize responses, optimize processing time, and improve the user experience.

Results that the reader will obtain.

- Deep understanding of the role of prompts in AI

- Mastery of techniques to create effective prompts

- Ability to identify risks and avoid errors in interactions with AI models

- Tools to improve personalization and contextualization of AI-based systems

- Historical knowledge of the evolution of prompts and their main technological innovations

AI is advancing rapidly, and prompt engineering stands as a vital piece in this technological puzzle. By studying the fundamentals presented in this book, the reader acquires not only technical knowledge, but also the ability to shape future interactions between humans and machines.

Happy reading and a journey full of discoveries.

Prof. Marcão - Marcus Vinícius Pinto

M. Sc. in Information Technology
Specialist in Information Technology.
Consultant, Mentor and Speaker on Artificial Intelligence,
Information Architecture and Data Governance.
Founder, CEO, teacher and
pedagogical advisor at MVP Consult.

1   Fundamentals of artificial intelligence.

Artificial Intelligence (AI), at its core, refers to systems or machines that mimic human intelligence to perform tasks and progressively improve based on the information they gather.

This multidisciplinary field crosses areas such as computer science, psychology, philosophy, neuroscience, among others, to create machines capable of reasoning, perception and learning.

1.1   AI applications.

The applications of AI are diverse and cut across all sectors of society, including:

1. Health. Faster and more accurate diagnoses, predictions of disease outbreaks, personalization of treatments, and automation of administrative tasks.

2. Transport. Autonomous vehicles, route optimization and traffic management.

3. Finance. Fraud detection systems, risk management, robo-advisors for investment advice and operations automation.

4. Retail. Personalization of the customer experience, optimization of inventory, and prediction of market trends.

5. Manufacturing. Predictive equipment maintenance, supply chain management, and production line automation.

1.2   Data Requirements for AI.

For AI systems to work and learn, they need data, often in large quantities. This data is used to train machine learning algorithms, which are the heart of most AI applications.

The fundamental pillars on the data requirements for AI include.

1. Volume of data. AI, especially deep learning, requires large volumes of data to identify patterns and make accurate predictions. This is often referred to as 'big data'.

2. Data quality. The quality of the data influences the accuracy of the AI's results. This encompasses the accuracy, completeness, relevance, and timeliness of the data.

3. Variety of data. AI needs a variety of data to capture the complexity of the real world and offer very generalized results. This includes structured data (such as database tables), unstructured data (such as free text, images, audio, and video), and semi-structured data (such as emails or formatted documents).

4. Labeled data. For supervised learning methods, it's crucial to have labeled data, that is, data where observations are linked to known labels or responses that the algorithm can use to learn and make predictions.

5. Diversity of data. The data should cover a diverse range of cases and scenarios in order to reduce bias and ensure that AI can function properly under diverse conditions.

6. Shareable data. Privacy and legality issues must be considered to ensure that data can be shared with AI systems ethically and in accordance with current regulations, such as GDPR.

7. Data recorded temporarily. For problems such as time series analysis or when the chronology is significant, the data needs to be correctly annotated with timestamps.

Data quality and variety are key to avoiding the problem of 'garbage in, garbage out' (GIGO), where low-quality input data in AI training leads to low-quality results.

It is essential that the data used in the training not only fairly represents all affected groups, but is also free from bias that could lead to discrimination or injustice.

In addition to data, AI systems also require advanced algorithms, powerful computer architecture (such as specialized GPUs for processing neural networks), and software frameworks and mathematical libraries that enable the deployment and training of AI models.

1.3   AI Development and Training

Developing an AI system requires clear problem definition, data collection and cleaning, choosing a suitable machine learning model, training the model with a dataset, and evaluating its effectiveness.

Once trained, the AI model is tested with a new dataset (the test set) to verify its ability to generalize and make predictions or make decisions based on previously unseen data.

There are several methods and techniques used in the AI training process, including:

1. Supervised learning. Where models are trained on a dataset with known labels. They learn to predict output from the inputs provided.

2. Unsupervised learning. Where models look for patterns in labelless data, such as customer segmentation in marketing.

3. Reinforcement learning. A model learns through trial and error, maximizing a reward or minimizing a punishment during training.

4. Neural networks and deep learning. Complex structures that mimic the way the human brain processes information, effective especially in tasks such as speech and image recognition.

1.4   Challenges of AI.

Despite significant progress in AI, several challenges remain, including:

1. Bias and Justice. AI systems can perpetuate or even amplify biases present in training data.

2. Explainability and Transparency. Many AI models, especially deep neural networks, are considered 'black boxes' and offer little understanding of how decisions are made.

3. Data Privacy. AI models can reveal sensitive or personal information contained in the training data.

4. Safety. AI systems can be vulnerable to attacks, such as examples of adversity designed to fool AI models.

1.5   Guidelines for creating meaningful interactions.

1.5.1   The importance of personalization and contextualization.

Prompt engineering, within the context of modern digital interactions, takes a leading role as a tool for aligning artificial intelligence (AI) and human needs.

This sophisticated practice represents the meticulous art of modeling questions, commands, or instructions to extract desired answers from an AI system, or to guide the user experience in an intuitive and effective way.

The core of this approach is based on personalization and contextualization, two essential pillars for building productive dialogues and meaningful interactions between man and machine.

Personalization refers to fine-tuning prompts so that they reflect individual interests, historical preferences, and specific user needs.

This goes beyond the use of generic demographics; it requires understanding the nuances of the individual's behavior and expectations. By doing so, a more synergistic and natural experience is created, where the technology becomes an extension of the user's thinking and intentions.

On the other hand, contextualization concerns the incorporation of the user's current environment and circumstances into prompt engineering. This involves not only analyzing where and when the user is interacting with the system, but also understanding their emotional and social situation.

An AI capable of discerning such aspects can offer more accurate answers and suggestions, elevating the quality of the interaction beyond basic functionality to a truly enriching experience.

The processes of personalization and contextualization in prompt engineering translate into tangible benefits, not only for users, but also for the entities that implement such systems.

Users enjoy more intuitive and appropriate services, which naturally leads to greater satisfaction and loyalty. For companies and developers, this means increased engagement, reduced handle times, and potentially higher conversions if applicable to the business context or services offered.

By adjusting AI-powered interactions to reflect real-time circumstances and user dynamics, organizations can achieve truly two-way communication, where technology responds and elicits stimuli that make sense for each individual user.

1.5.2   Consistency, simplicity and accessibility.

The importance of consistency, simplicity, and accessibility in prompt engineering is critical to creating interactions that are both intuitive and satisfying for users.

These principles are vital to ensure that technological products can be used efficiently and without frustration, regardless of the user's experience or technical ability.

Consistency means that prompts should follow a recognizable pattern, allowing users to develop an intuition about how to interact with the interface without having to relearn at each step.

Whether it's prompts, mobile apps, websites, or AI systems, consistency helps build trust and allows users to focus on the task at hand rather than deciphering the interface at every moment.

For example, if a voice command prompt for a smart assistant responds differently to similar commands, it can confuse the user.

Case studies on the usability of intelligent assistants often highlight the need for consistency in the responses and behavior of these systems.

Simplicity, on the other hand, is linked to clarity and ease of use. Simple, straightforward prompts are easier to understand and less likely to cause errors.

This does not mean that the complexity of the system should be reduced, but that the complexity should not overwhelm the user.

The design of an automated teller machine (ATM) is a classic example where simplicity is essential. Although behind each operation there is a complex banking system, the interaction for the user is done through clear instructions and easy-to-follow steps.

Accessibility refers to the ability of all users, including those with disabilities, to be able to use the system. This is critical to ensure that no one is excluded from digital interaction. A good example in this case is the design of websites that follow the WCAG (Web Content Accessibility Guidelines) guidelines.

Case studies looking at website redesigns can show how implementing high contrast between text and background, the use of tags on images, and keyboard navigation features not only benefit visually impaired users, but also improve the overall experience for everyone.

2 Structuring concepts: unraveling the mysteries of prompt engineering.

In the context of artificial intelligence, prompt engineering emerges as a powerful tool for us to master the potential of language models.

In artificial intelligence, a "prompt" refers to an instruction or suggestion provided to the AI model to direct its text generation.

The prompt is a specific input given to the model to influence the response it will generate. It can be a sentence, a question, a command, or any other piece of information that serves as a starting point for text generation by the AI model.

The use of prompts is commonly found in natural language processing applications such as chatbots, virtual assistants, and text generation systems.

Through the formulation of precise and effective instructions, this discipline allows shaping the behavior of these systems, guiding them in generating relevant, informative, and creative responses.

2.1 What is Prompt Engineering?

"Prompt engineering" is a practice in the field of artificial intelligence that involves carefully choosing and adjusting prompts to direct the behavior of AI models.

This technique aims to optimize an AI model's ability to generate accurate and relevant responses in conjunction with a specific prompt.

Prompt engineering is especially useful in language models, such as Generative Pre-trained Transformer (GPT) models, where the choice of prompt can significantly influence the quality of the output generated by the model.

Prompt engineers can adjust the prompt wording, choice of keywords, question structure, and other settings to get more appropriate and coherent answers.

Unlike traditional machine learning models, Large Language Models (LLMs) offer the unique ability to provide new insights without the need for retraining.

This innovation catalyzed a transformative wave, allowing individuals to effortlessly program computers through simple text instructions.

Prompt engineering is a technique for directing an LLM's responses to specific outcomes without changing the model's weights or parameters, relying solely on strategic in-context statements. This entails the art of effectively communicating with AI to achieve the desired results.

This method is applied across a spectrum of tasks, ranging from questions and answers to arithmetic reasoning. It serves as a tool for exploring the limits and potentials of LLMs.

2.2   Core Elements of Prompt Engineering.

The core elements of prompt engineering focus on optimizing the interaction between an artificial intelligence model and the user, through the proper formulation of prompts that direct the model's behavior.

Careful prompt choice is essential for getting accurate and relevant results from the AI model, providing more effective and natural communication.

Prompt engineering involves understanding the purpose of the interaction, defining clear and appropriate language, identifying keywords or key concepts that the model should consider, and crafting a prompt structure that guides the desired response.

Thus, it is possible to adjust and personalize the interaction with AI models, maximizing its ability to understand and generate relevant responses.

Prompt engineering is an essential practice for ensuring that AI models meet user needs and provide accurate and useful results across a wide variety of applications.

Several researchers and authors have contributed to the advancement of prompt engineering, offering valuable insights into this ever-developing area.

Some authors who stand out in this context are Yannic Kilcher, Scott Reed, Emily M. Bender, Liu Pengfei and Elvis Saraiva.

In a traditional supervised learning system for NLP (Natural Language Processing), a formal prompt description would be to assume an input x, usually text, and predict an output y based on a model $P(y|x; \theta)$. y can be a label, text, or other output variety.

To learn the parameters θ of this model, we use a dataset containing input and output pairs, and train a model to predict this conditional probability. Let's illustrate this with two stereotypical examples.

First, text classification records an input text x and predicts a label y from a fixed set of labels Y. For example, sentiment analysis (Pang et al., 2002; Socher et al., 2013) assume an input x = "I love this movie." and predict a label y = ++, from a set of labels Y = {++, +, ~, -, --}.

Second, conditional text generation takes an input x and generates another text y. An example is machine translation (Koehn, 2009), where the input is text in a language, such as Finnish x = "Hyvää huomenta." and the output is English y = "Good morning.".

2.3   An effective prompt.

An effective prompt should be:

- Clear and Concise. The prompt should be written clearly and concisely, avoiding ambiguity and unnecessary terms. This makes it easier to understand the language model and ensures that it focuses on the most relevant aspects of the task.

- Informative and Contextualized. The prompt should provide the language model with all the information relevant to the execution of the task. This includes data, examples, and specific instructions on what is expected of the model.

- Adapted to the Domain. The prompt should be tailored to the domain of the task at hand. This means using specific terminology and incorporating contextual knowledge relevant to the language model to perform well.

Prompt engineering opens up a range of possibilities for the use of language models, going beyond the simple translation of texts.

Through creative and challenging prompts, the prompt engineer can stimulate the generation of.

- Poems. Imagine a prompt engineer inspiring a language model to create poems that express the deepest emotions of the human soul.

- Scripts. Prompt engineering opens doors for the creation of engaging and original cinematic scripts, driving the entertainment industry forward.

- Songs. The art of formulating prompts allows you to compose songs that delight the ears and touch the heart, taking the musical experience to a new level.

- Creative Content. Prompt engineering makes it possible to generate a variety of creative content, from advertising to informative blog articles.

2.4   Benefits of Prompt Engineering.

Adopting prompt engineering brings with it a range of benefits that significantly enhance the language model experience:

- Greater Control and Predictability. Prompt engineering gives the user greater control over the behavior of the language model, allowing them to achieve more accurate and predictable results.

- Expanding Creative Possibilities. Through prompt engineering, language models become powerful tools for creating creative and original content, opening up new frontiers for artistic expression and communication.

- Improved Communication and Collaboration. Prompt engineering facilitates communication between humans and language models, allowing for more effective and productive collaboration across multiple tasks.

- Increased Efficiency and Productivity. By directing the language model to specific tasks, prompt engineering contributes to increased efficiency and productivity, optimizing the time and resources used.

2.5   Objectives of Prompt Engineering.

Prompt engineering pursues several goals that aim to improve the performance and versatility of language models.

Among the main objectives, we can highlight:
- Increase the Accuracy and Relevance of Responses. Through well-structured prompts, the prompt engineer ensures that the language model focuses on the most relevant aspects of the task at hand, avoiding irrelevant or inaccurate answers.

- Improve Text Fluency and Coherence. Prompt engineering contributes to the generation of more fluid and cohesive texts, free of grammatical errors and inconsistencies. The prompt engineer shapes the style and structure of the text, ensuring that communication is clear and enjoyable to the reader.

- Promote Creativity and Originality. Prompt engineering opens doors to exploring the creativity of language models.

  Through challenging and inspiring prompts, the prompt engineer can stimulate the generation of poems, scripts, songs, and other creative content with a high level of originality.
- Adapt the Model to Different Domains. Prompt engineering allows you to adapt the language model to meet the needs of different areas of knowledge.

  Through the use of specific terminology and the incorporation of contextual knowledge, the prompt engineer ensures that the model operates efficiently in a variety of domains, from medicine to law.

2.6   Requirements to be a successful prompt engineer.

To be a successful prompt engineer, a specific set of skills and attributes is required, involving technical, creative, and analytical competencies.

Below are the key requirements that someone aspiring to this position must meet or seek to develop.

1. Strong Understanding of AI and Language Models.

- Deep knowledge of how text production models such as GPT-4 work.

- Understanding of the principles of machine learning and neural networks.

2. Programming Skills.

- Familiarity with programming languages relevant to working with AI, such as Python.

- Ability to work with AI APIs and systems integration.

3. Effective Prompt Formulation Capabilities.

- Ability to write clear, concise, and targeted prompts that induce the AI to generate the desired output.

- Understanding how different formulations can influence the results generated by the model.

4. Analytical Skills.

- Ability to analyze and interpret AI outputs to ensure accuracy and relevance.

- Ability to adjust and refine prompts based on results for continuous improvement.

5. Knowledge of AI Ethics and Bias Considerations.

- Awareness of ethics in AI and the social impacts of technology.

- Commitment to promoting equity and avoiding the reinforcement of stereotypes or prejudices.

6. Creativity and Problem Solving.

- Creativity to explore new ways to interact with AI and to solve unusual problems.

- Ability to think outside the box and develop innovative prompts that overcome specific challenges.

7. Excellent Communication and Interdisciplinary Collaboration.

- The ability to communicate effectively with a multidisciplinary team, including computer scientists, content specialists, and stakeholders.

- Ability to collaborate with other professionals to develop AI interaction strategies that are efficient and effective.

8. Commitment to Continuous Learning.

- As the field of artificial intelligence is constantly evolving, a commitment to continuous learning is crucial to stay up-to-date with the latest trends and techniques.

- Flexibility to adapt to new tools, technologies, and methods as they emerge in the field of AI.

9. Project Management and Organization.

- Ability to manage multiple projects and prioritize tasks in dynamic environments and often with tight deadlines.

- Detailed attention and organizational skills to document work processes and results in a systematic manner.

10. Focus on the User and Empathy.

- The prompt design should always keep the end user in mind; understanding their needs and how interacting with AI can solve their problems is essential.

- Ability to put yourself in the user's shoes to create experiences that are intuitive and satisfying.

11. Ability to Test and Iterate.

- I strive to test the prompts extensively to identify flaws or areas for improvement.

- Willingness to iterate on feedback and results, continually refining the quality and effectiveness of interactions.

12. Emotional Intelligence.

- Ability to manage your own emotions and understand the emotions of others to improve collaboration with the team and the creation of prompts that resonate with users.

Being a prompt engineer requires a combination of technical skills and interpersonal skills. Successful prompt engineering is not just about understanding the intricacies of the AI model, but also about applying that knowledge ethically and responsibly to create interactions that are beneficial, clear, and accessible for all users.

2.7   Risks of having incorrect prompts.

Creating incorrect or poorly worded prompts can carry a number of risks and negative implications both in controlled environments and in practical use by end users.

Below I detail the main risks associated with incorrect prompts in interactions with natural language-based artificial intelligence systems, such as GPT-4.

1. Inaccurate or Irrelevant Results.

- Poorly crafted prompts can lead to responses that don't match the user's intent, becoming useless or, worse, providing incorrect information that can be used inappropriately.

2. Communication Failures.

- Ineffective communication through the prompt can result in misunderstandings, especially in critical situations where precise and clear instructions are essential.

3. Prejudice to Data-Driven Decisions.

- If the outputs generated by the system are based on incorrect prompts, the decisions made from this data can be flawed, leading to undesirable consequences in business situations, research, or even in the context of public safety.

4. Bias and Discrimination.

- Prompts that inadvertently reinforce stereotypes or prejudices can perpetuate biases and lead to discrimination, undermining ethical and legal principles.

5. Impacts on Education and Learning.

- In the educational context, incorrect prompts can lead to mistaken learning, solidifying misconceptions and hindering the educational process.

6. Wear and Tear of User Trust.

- The consistency of inaccurate or irrelevant results can erode users' confidence in the effectiveness of AI, hindering the adoption and uptake of useful technologies.

7. Increased operating costs.

- In the business sphere, additional time and resources may be required to correct the impacts of outputs generated by inappropriate prompts, which generates an indirect cost and decreases operational efficiency.

8. Legal and Compliance Risks.

- Poorly constructed prompts that lead AI to generate content that is defamatory, invasive, or in violation of regulations can expose organizations to legal risks and consequent sanctions.

9. Compromised Security.

- In the context of cybersecurity, inappropriate prompts can result in the generation of sensitive information or improper data handling, opening loopholes for attacks or information leaks.

10. Negative Public Perceptions.

- Audiences may develop a negative view of AI and technology in general if they are frequently exposed to frustrating or offensive results derived from poorly worded prompts.

11. Cognitive Overload.

- Users may suffer from cognitive overload when trying to interpret and correct unexpected or confusing results, decreasing the usability of the system.

12. Adverse Social Impacts.

- If used on a large scale, AI with poorly calibrated prompts can reinforce harmful beliefs or spread misinformation, with the potential to negatively affect public discourse and social cohesion.

Prioritizing accuracy and clarity in prompt engineering is therefore vital to maximize the benefits and minimize the risks associated with using AI technology.

Investing time and resources in designing, testing, and refining prompts can help prevent many of the above negative consequences and ensure effective and safe interaction with artificial intelligence technologies.

3   History of prompt engineering.

Engineering is a science and art that shapes the world around us. From the earliest stone tools to the complex artificial intelligence systems of modern times, engineering has been a driving force behind humanity's progress.

However, when discussing the history of engineering, it is important to understand the various phases and innovations that have marked this path.

The history of engineering can be traced back to the great ancient civilizations. The Egyptians, for example, were proficient engineers, as the impressive constructions of the pyramids attest.

"No act of faith was necessary for the construction of the pyramids; science and engineering were sufficient" (Lewis, 1993). The Romans also left a legacy of engineering, including aqueducts, roads, and large structures like the Colosseum.

With the Renaissance and the Enlightenment, engineering began to formalize itself as a field of study. Personalities such as Leonardo da Vinci and Galileo Galilei manifested the intersection of art and science, with Da Vinci being known for his notebook of inventions that are works of engineering in essence.

The industrial revolution brought with it an explosion of advances in engineering. James Watt and his improvement in the steam engine were fundamental to this era, providing the development of factories and, consequently, urban growth.

"Watt's work in the development of the steam engine marking the transition from the age of iron tools to the age of machines."

In the twentieth century, engineering witnessed incredible advances in several areas such as automobiles, aerospace, and computing. Henry Ford revolutionized mass production with the assembly line, which signified a new era for production engineering.

In the early days of AI, human-machine interaction was rudimentary, limited to simple commands and predefined responses.

Alan Turing, one of the forerunners of AI, explored the idea of "intelligent machines" in his famous 1950 paper, "Computing Machinery and Intelligence." However, natural and intuitive communication with machines was still a distant dream.

With the advancement of NLP in the 1960s, the first chatbots emerged, programs capable of simulating conversations with humans. Joseph Weizenbaum, one of the pioneers in this area, created ELIZA in 1966, a chatbot that used pattern-matching rules to generate responses. Despite the limitations, ELIZA demonstrated the potential of AI to simulate human interaction.

The 1970s were marked by the rise of symbolic artificial intelligence, which sought to represent knowledge and reasoning through symbols and rules.

John McCarthy, a leading proponent of this approach, coined the term "artificial intelligence" in 1955. Symbolic systems such as SHRDLU, developed by Terry Winograd in 1970, have demonstrated AI's ability to manipulate symbols and perform complex tasks.

The late 20th and early 21st centuries saw an explosion of interest in machine learning and neural networks. These techniques have allowed AI systems to learn from data and make predictions without the need for explicit programming.

Figures such as Geoffrey Hinton, Yann LeCun, and Yoshua Bengio have led the deep learning renaissance, paving the way for the development of increasingly sophisticated language models.

It is possible to state without exaggeration that the current world, in which we find ourselves surrounded by a multiplicity of techno-scientific phenomena, owes its existence to the pioneering contributions of engineers.

Software engineering has also become a critical area, as reliance on technology has grown exponentially. Authors such as Frederick Brooks, in his classic book "The Mythical Man-Month", address challenges and best practices in software project management.

According to Brooks, "adding features to a delayed software project only makes it more backward" (Brooks et al., 2002).

Today, engineering promises to continue evolving and shaping the future. With a focus on sustainability, artificial intelligence, robotics, and other emerging areas, engineers have a key role to play in solving the challenges of the twenty-first century.

PROMPT engineering, in the context of artificial intelligence, is an area in constant evolution and relevance today. The combination of project management techniques with the application of artificial intelligence has revolutionized the way organizations manage and execute their initiatives.

To understand the history and impact of PROMPT engineering in the field of artificial intelligence, it is essential to explore the contributions of diverse experts and scholars over time.

The use of artificial intelligence in PROMPT engineering has been increasingly widespread, introducing innovative methods and tools for effective project management.

The author Peter Norvig, in his book "Artificial Intelligence: Structures and Strategies for Solving Complex Problems", points out that "artificial intelligence is the branch of computer science that deals with systems that "think" in a similar way to human beings" (Norvig, 2017).

This definition highlights the ability of artificial intelligence to automate complex tasks and improve decision-making.

In the context of PROMPT engineering, artificial intelligence plays a key role in identifying patterns, analyzing data, and supporting strategic decision-making.

Authors such as Stuart Russell and Peter Norvig, in their work "Artificial Intelligence", address the importance of machine learning and predictive algorithms in the engineering of intelligent systems (Russell & Norvig, 2016).

The application of artificial intelligence techniques makes it possible to optimize processes, anticipate problems, and improve the performance of engineering projects.

Throughout the history of PROMPT engineering in the context of artificial intelligence, we have seen significant advancements driven by the intersection between project management and technology.

Authors such as Ronald Howard and Howard D. Morgan, in their book "Decision Analysis in Management: A Comprehensive Guide to Modeling, Analysis, and Applications", explore analytical methods for decision-making in complex environments, highlighting the importance of artificial intelligence in modeling scenarios and evaluating alternatives.

The evolution of PROMPT engineering in the context of artificial intelligence is also evidenced by the impact of automation and robotics on production processes.

Authors such as John Craig (2017), in his book "Introduction to Robotics: Mechanics and Control", addresses the intersection between robotics, artificial intelligence, and systems engineering, highlighting the technological advances that make it possible to automate complex tasks.

The integration of intelligent robotic systems in PROMPT engineering has facilitated the performance of repetitive activities and improved operational efficiency.

In the current landscape, PROMPT engineering continues to develop, driven by the increasing demand for innovative and effective solutions.

With the advent of big data analytics, artificial intelligence, and automation, it is essential for engineering professionals to be up-to-date with the latest technologies and methodologies to ensure the success of their projects.

Prompt engineering refers to the art and science of formulating questions and prompts that direct artificial intelligence (AI) systems, such as OpenAI's language models, to generate useful and accurate answers or content.

This discipline has gained importance with the advancement of AI technologies, especially after the emergence of increasingly sophisticated models, such as OpenAI's GPT model series.

The history of prompt engineering is intrinsically linked to advances in understanding how AI systems process and respond to natural language.

Already in the 50s and 60s, with the first works in artificial intelligence, such as that of Alan Turing, the idea of communicating with a machine using natural language was already an explored concept.

However, it was only with the proliferation of large language models such as GPT-3 and the subsequent GPT-4 that prompt engineering became a crucial facet of human interaction with AI.

OpenAI's GPT-3 researchers noted the model's sensitivity to small variations in prompts and how this could dramatically affect the quality of the outputs (Brown et al., "Language Models are Few-Shot Learners," 2020).

The curiosities surrounding prompt engineering include the fact that practitioners of this discipline learn not only how to communicate effectively with AI, but also how to understand its limitations and peculiarities.

There is an element of "art" to this practice, since certain strategies work better in specific situations; For example, prompts that mimic teaching situations or that use analogies tend to guide the model to deeper understanding displays.

This may be related to Vygotsky's work on the "Zone of Proximal Development", in which he suggests that learning occurs most effectively when it is slightly beyond the student's current level of independence (Vygotsky, 1978).

Similarly, in prompt engineering, formulating questions that push the boundaries of AI's understanding can lead to more sophisticated responses.

Another curious aspect is that, as our ability to interact with AI improves through prompt engineering, we also develop a better understanding of the very nature of human language processing.

It's almost as if a mirror effect is occurring: by teaching AI how to understand and respond to our language, we learn a lot about how we ourselves communicate and process information.

It is an interdisciplinary field that crosses lines between linguistics, cognitive psychology, computer science, and even philosophy.

To talk about curiosities in prompt engineering is also to mention the ethical and social challenges that arise. With the power to influence the output of AI, it is often questioned who has control over these systems and how they can be used or misused.

Selbst et al. (2019) discussed these concerns from a fairness and equality perspective in "Fairness and Abstraction in Sociotechnical Systems" (2019), underscoring the importance of transparency and accountability in prompt creation.

Prompt engineering has become an essential skill not only for researchers and developers working directly with AIs, but also for users who want to extract the most value from these advanced tools.

As the field of AI continues to evolve, prompt engineering can be expected to evolve as well, perhaps becoming a discipline of its own with more formalized methods and theories.

In recent years, we have witnessed the emergence of large language models (LLMs), such as GPT-3 and LaMDA, which demonstrate impressive capabilities to generate text, translate languages, and write different types of creative content.

Prompt engineering has become crucial in unlocking the full potential of these models, allowing users to target them accurately and achieve high-quality results.

Pioneers of Prompt Engineering and their Contributions:

- Robin Kearon. It defined the basic principles of prompt engineering and explored its potential to improve human-computer interaction.

- Emily M Bender and Alexander Rush. They developed techniques to optimize prompts and evaluate the quality of responses generated by LLMs.

- Scott Reed et al.. They introduced the concept of "prompt programming", demonstrating how prompts can be used to program LLMs to perform complex tasks.

Prompt engineering has a wide range of applications in a variety of industries, including:

- Content Generation. Creation of informative texts, articles, scripts, poems and other formats of creative content.

- Machine translation. Accurate and fluid translation of texts between different languages.

- Customer Service. Automating customer service tasks, answering questions and resolving issues efficiently.

- Software Development. Assistance in coding, test generation and software documentation.

3.1   Applications of Prompt Engineering.

Prompt engineering, as an emerging field associated with advances in artificial intelligence, has a wide range of applications in several areas.

Some of these applications are:

1. Educational Technology. Prompt engineering is used to create interactive learning environments. Examples include learning assistants that help students understand complex concepts through interactive dialogues tailored to their level of knowledge and learning style, as well as programming tutorials and mathematical problem-solving that guide them step by step.

2. Customer Service. Many businesses utilize AI-powered chatbots that rely heavily on prompt engineering to interact with customers. These systems can manage bookings, provide technical support, or even offer personalized shopping advice, depending on how the prompts are built to guide the conversation.

3. Health Area. In healthcare, prompt engineering can be used to create clinical data analysis systems. AI can be fed with a detailed prompt to identify patterns in electronic medical records, helping with the prediction of disease outbreaks or the personalization of treatment plans.

4. Content Creation. Journalists, writers, and marketers use prompt engineering to generate articles, creative stories, or social media content. With carefully designed prompts, AI can

first produce drafts or ideas that will serve as the basis for original and engaging content.

5. Software Development. Software engineers can use prompts to generate pseudocode or even complete source code in some instances, depending on the complexity of the task. These systems can also be used for debugging, where the prompt guides the AI in identifying errors in the code.

6. Research and Data Analysis. Data scientists can formulate prompts to instruct AI to analyze large data sets, identifying trends, patterns, and anomalies. Prompt engineering here streamlines the insights process by allowing professionals to formulate specific hypotheses or questions that would be analyzed by the machine, making it easier to discover relevant information amidst a sea of data.

7. Translation and Linguistics. Prompt engineering plays a significant role in machine translation and natural language processing. A well-worded prompt can direct the system to understand the desired context and tone, resulting in more accurate and natural translations, especially useful for communication in globalized companies or social media platforms.

8. Games and Entertainment. Video game and interactive content creators can utilize prompt engineering to develop branching narratives and dialogue with AI-controlled characters. Prompts help ensure that these interactions are coherent and engaging, providing a richer user experience.

9. Cybersecurity. In the field of cybersecurity, prompts can be designed to help AI systems monitor networks for suspicious activity, filter out phishing, and other threats. The ability to naturally process language allows AI to identify and alert on threats in real-time.

10. Legal. Artificial intelligence and prompt engineering are transforming the way lawyers work by facilitating legal research and document analysis. AI can be instructed to look for relevant precedents and legislation, helping to build cases or interpret legal nuances more efficiently.

11. Human resources. Companies use AI to screen candidates and to help make hiring decisions. The prompts here direct the AI to evaluate CVs and candidate profiles against the requirements of a vacancy, optimizing the recruitment process.

Prompt engineering, when applied correctly, offers a number of considerable advantages in many areas of artificial intelligence application, but as with any powerful technology, it also carries with it intrinsic risks that must be carefully managed.

3.2   Advantages and risks.

Advantages of Prompt Engineering:

1. Efficiency and Scalability. Utilizing prompt engineering in AI allows you to automate tasks that would traditionally require human intervention, such as customer service or data analysis, providing quick and scalable responses to complex problems.

2. Personalization and Relevance. Prompts can be tailored to offer personalized responses, increasing the relevance and effectiveness of the services and products offered. This is particularly beneficial in areas such as education and healthcare, where customized solutions can make a big difference.

3. Cost Reduction. By automating repetitive and time-consuming tasks, prompt engineering can reduce operational costs. This is evident in industries such as legal and human resources, where the initial screening of information can be significantly accelerated.

4. Improved Decision Making. The ability to quickly process and analyze large amounts of data can lead to better business and scientific decisions. Researchers and analysts have the advantage of gaining more deeply informed, data-driven insights.

Risks of Prompt Engineering:

1. Bias and Discrimination. If prompts aren't carefully designed to avoid bias, AIs can generate or even amplify existing biases in data or human behavior. This is particularly concerning in areas of high responsibility such as human resources and justice.

2. Manipulation and Disinformation. The same ability that allows AI to create informative and relevant content can be misused to generate misinformation or manipulative content, especially when induced by malicious prompts.

3. Over-Reliance on Technology. Over-reliance on AI systems for decision-making can lead to a loss of human autonomy and judgment. In areas such as health and law, it is essential that AI is used as a support tool, and not as a substitute for human discernment.

4. Data Privacy and Security. The collection and analysis of large volumes of data through prompt engineering raises significant concerns about privacy and security. If systems are compromised, sensitive information can be exposed, resulting in severe consequences for individuals and organizations.

To mitigate these risks and maximize the advantages of prompt engineering, it is essential to implement rigorous data security practices, transparency in the use of AI, proper human oversight, and ensuring compliance with current regulations, such as the General Data Protection Law (LGPD).

Additionally, awareness and education about the potential impacts of AI are key to ensuring that its use is ethical and responsible.

Prompt engineering is a powerful tool that presents many opportunities to enhance and transform various areas of expertise. However, it is crucial to address the risks associated with its use proactively and cautiously, aiming to ensure long-term benefits and promote a responsible and sustainable innovation environment.

3.3   The historical trail.

The history of language models is a backdrop of mathematical and computational progress, painstakingly woven over the past few decades by a dedicated community of linguists, computer scientists, and artificial intelligence researchers.

From the earliest rule-based models to modern deep neural networks, the journey of language models reflects the very evolution of machines to process and understand complex human languages.

Fast forward to the 1960s, and the dominant approach to natural language processing was centered on systems based on grammatical rules.

Noam Chomsky in his seminal work "Syntactic Structures" (1957), introduced the idea of generative grammars, which became central to the field of computational linguistics.

Chomsky argued that the underlying structure of language could be modeled by a finite set of rules.

However, the problem with the rules was their rigidity. They couldn't cope well with the ambiguity and natural variability of human language.

This dilemma has been pointed out by researchers such as Terry Winograd, who demonstrated, in his SHRDLU system (1972), that computer understanding of natural language requires more than successful grammar rules, the machine also needs to understand the context in which the language is being used.

The turn of the millennium saw a growth in the use of statistical approaches to language models, typical of corpus linguistics and support vector machines.

Researchers like Frederick Jelinek at IBM have played a revolutionary role in embracing statistical models in natural language processing.

Jelinek, often quoted for his provocative statement "Every time I fire a linguist, the performance of our speech recognition system goes up," emphasized the virtues of data-driven approaches rather than manual rules.

The 1990s saw the arrival of the so-called vector space model, an approach that represented words in multidimensional spaces, capturing semantic and syntactic relationships through co-occurrence in large sets of text.

These ideas were the prelude to word embedding approaches, such as those presented by researcher Tomas Mikolov and collaborators in their series of papers on the Word2Vec technique in 2013, who proposed an effective method for learning vector representations for words from a corpus of text.

It is in the last ten years that the history of language models really accelerates. We were introduced to models such as Long Short-Term Memory (LSTM), introduced by Sepp Hochreiter and in 1997, which addressed problems related to memory in long sequences, a significant advance for NLP and sequence applications in general.

However, it was with the innovation of deep neural networks, and in particular the "Transformer" model, proposed by Vaswani et al. in the 2017 paper "Attention is All You Need", that opened doors for significant advances in language models.

Transformers and the idea of selective attention proved revolutionary, enabling models such as BERT (Bidirectional Encoder Representations from Transformers) by Jacob Devlin and his team in 2018, which became a milestone in the field by allowing a language model to take into account the full context of a word (in both directions) for its representation.

This advancement has provided text comprehension and fine-tuning capabilities in specific NLP tasks like never before.

More recently, with the evolution of transformers, we have seen the rise of even more powerful and larger-scale models, such as GPT (Generative Pretrained Transformer) developed by OpenAI.

Following its advances, the publication of "Language Models are Few-Shot Learners" by OpenAI researchers in 2020 introduced GPT-3, which performs remarkably well on several NLP tasks with virtually no task-specific adjustments, a feat known as few-shot learning.

These models, particularly BERT and GPT-3, highlight the potential of the approach known as transfer learning, where the ability gained in learning one task is transferred to improve learning in another.

As Yann LeCun, a pioneer in convolutional neural networks, pointed out, "The biggest advances in AI and machine learning have come not only from supervised learning, but from transfer learning, where a system learns a task and applies that knowledge to related tasks."

With the unbridled growth in computing power and the unprecedented availability of large-scale data, these language models have been trained on corpus of texts spanning billions of words, absorbing the subtlest linguistic patterns, grammar, style, and even thematic content found in books, articles, websites, and others.

The amount of data and processing power allowed for a qualitative leap in NLP that, just a decade ago, might have seemed like science fiction.

While the journey has been long and full of groundbreaking breakthroughs, researchers continue to face significant challenges. Although models like GPT-3 can generate texts that are indistinguishable from those written by humans in many cases, they can still struggle with common-sense notions and complex inference.

As Bengio, one of the leading names in contemporary AI, has pointed out on several occasions, understanding language at a deeper level that transcends pure statistics is still an open frontier.

The next step involves understanding and replicating human reasoning, the ability to handle abstract knowledge, and the application of general intelligence to natural language processing.

In this sense, the most recent focus has migrated to models that not only process language, but are also capable of making logical inferences and deductions.

The integration of NLP with symbolic or hybrid systems and the growing research in language understanding and reasoning are examples of this trend.

On the other hand, growing concerns about the ethics of AI have also come to the fore. Julia Hirschberg, a pioneer in the fields of prosody and vocal expression in NLP, highlighted the importance of ensuring that language models are fair and do not perpetuate stereotypes or bias.

The field has seen a significant increase in the attention paid to these ethical issues, aiming at creating more inclusive and representative models.

*The history of language models is not only a
narrative of technical innovation, but also one of
adaptation to social responsibility.*

The challenge now is to cultivate these advances in ways that benefit society broadly, by maintaining a constant dialogue about the implications of the technology we are creating, and by ensuring that the human voice – in all its forms and variations – remains at the heart of artificial communication and understanding.

As Geoff Hinton, another prominent figure in AI and neural networks, points out, we are witnessing paradigmatic shifts in how we approach artificial intelligence.

The era of 'heavy language models', which require a substantial amount of computational power and data, is certainly advancing our understanding and technical capability, but the scientific community is now striving for a balance where efficiency, effectiveness, and ethics are equally valued.

We are approaching a future where language models can form the backbone of not only specific NLP applications, but also broader and more sophisticated AI systems.

The view put forward by Demis Hassabis, co-founder of DeepMind, is that we are moving towards AI systems that can learn more efficiently and flexibly, suggesting that the future of language models will go beyond simple classification tasks and will be able to perform creative and cognitively complex tasks with little or no human intervention.

But as we move in this direction, it is increasingly evident that collaboration across disciplines is crucial. Linguists, psychologists, philosophers, and ethicists are teaming up with engineers and computer scientists to grapple with the complexity of language and human cognition.

Through this interdisciplinary collaboration, the language models of the future will be more representative, conscious, and ethically aligned with society's values.

This holistic synthesis is well represented in the observation of Noam Chomsky, who despite his initial hesitation regarding statistical methods, recognized the contribution of these approaches to language processing.

The convergence between symbolic and statistical methods promises to usher in a new era of language models, where machine intelligence is not merely based on vast data sets, but also on a refined understanding of the underlying mechanisms of human cognition and communication.

In this sense, the history of language models is a continuous account of trial, error, and success, punctuated by numerous insights and advances.

It is a story that is still ongoing, with chapters being written each passing day as we as a society and scientific community explore the tremendous potential and address the intricate challenges that these technologies pose.

Advances in neural network architectures have been fundamental for the emergence and consolidation of significant advances in the field of Natural Language Processing (NLP).

Initial attempts to model human language through machine learning approaches faced significant hurdles due to the inherent complexity of temporal sequences and linguistic patterns. In this scenario, the evolution of neural networks has paved the way for great advances.

3.3.1   Recurrent Neural Networks (RNNs).

RNNs represent one of the first attempts at this advance. Unlike traditional neural networks, recurrent neural networks have the unique ability to process sequences of inputs with varying lengths, storing temporary information in the hidden state.

This is essential for NLP tasks such as translation and speech recognition, as it allows the network to maintain a degree of 'memory' over previous inputs.

However, classical RNNs are limited by the difficulty known as the vanishing gradient problem, which makes training RNNs in long sequences challenging.

In long sequences, the contribution of information from previous inputs becomes so minuscule that the model cannot learn long-range correlations effectively.

3.3.2   Long Short-Term Memory (LSTMs).

To overcome the limitations, researchers Sepp Hochreiter and Jürgen Schmidhuber presented the LSTM model in 1997. LSTMs incorporate mechanisms called gates, which regulate the flow of information, allowing the network to preserve long-term information and forget about unnecessary information.

These ports help alleviate the problem of gradient fading and have made LSTMs a popular choice for many NLP applications, such as machine translation, where significant parts of the context need to be retained over long strings of text.

3.3.3   Selective Attention.

Another major breakthrough in neural network architectures came with the introduction of the selective attention mechanism. Initially applied to machine translation tasks, the attention mechanism allowed models to focus on relevant parts of the input sequence when they produced the output sequence.

This simulates the way humans pay attention to different components of information when they are processing language.

Pioneering work involving attention architecture includes the 2014 paper "Neural Machine Translation by Jointly Learning to Align and Translate" by Dzmitry Bahdanau et al., which showed how incorporating attention into the model significantly improved its performance by allowing it to consider the full context of an input sentence when translating individual words.

3.3.4   Transformers and Self-Attention.

The notion of selective attention was later extended to the self-attention approach in Transformer architecture, proposed by Vaswani et al. in 2017.

In Transformer, the self-attention mechanism allows the entire input sequence to be processed simultaneously, unlike LSTMs and RNNs that process the sequences step-by-step. This led to major gains in efficiency and effectiveness when dealing with long distances of language dependence.

The Transformer architecture is fundamental in the structures of many of the next-generation language models, including BERT, GPT-3, and others. It allows models to capture the context of the entire sequence of tokens at once and has influenced virtually every aspect of modern NLP.

Advances in neural network architectures such as RNNs, LSTMs, and selective attention have opened up new horizons for NLP.

Not only have they empowered NLP systems to perform tasks with unprecedented accuracy and efficiency, but they have also paved the way for intrinsic language understanding that goes beyond mere superficial text analysis.

With LSTMs and subsequent advances, the NLP community began to face more complex problems, such as language generation, automatic summarization, named entity recognition, and many others.

The ability to understand and generate coherent and relevant text has become a palpable reality thanks to these innovations in neural networks.

Transformer, in particular, stood out for its parallelism capability, which drastically reduced the time it took to train models on large datasets.

The self-attention technique, which is central to Transformers, was a game-changer, eliminating the need for sequential recurrence and allowing the model to give different weights to different parts of the data input—a facet that proved extremely useful for capturing complex and subtle relationships in text.

Transformers are at the base of so-called "autoregressive" language models, which generate text by predicting the next word in the sequence, given all previous words.

These models have advanced to combine self-attention with massive training techniques, offering the ability to "learn" the structure and nuances of language from an immense volume of textual data.

The result of these advances has been NLP models that not only understand language at a sophisticated level, but can also adapt to new tasks with minimal intervention, a process known as "fine-tuning."

3.4   Current results.

Thus, with models such as BERT and GPT-3, researchers and engineers now have tools at hand that, once trained, can apply their learning to an incredible variety of NLP problems, extracting contextual knowledge that is essential for language comprehension and generation.

These modern neural network architectures continue to spur research and development in the field of NLP, driving the development of practical applications in various industries, including machine translation, intelligent dialogue systems, automatic text summarization, and the development of more intuitive personal agents.

The efficiency in the treatment of text sequences provided by Transformers has proven to be a starting point for continuous innovation, including the development of models that attempt to incorporate a deeper understanding of the world and common knowledge.

As Yann LeCun, one of the pioneers in the field of deep learning, commented, the ability to integrate world knowledge and reasoning is the next big challenge for NLP.

Current research is focused on even more advanced models that can perform logical inference and generalization across multiple domains. This is an exciting direction that could lead to more understandable and flexible AI systems that can interact, learn, and react in a more human-like way.

In addition to direct applications, advances in neural network architectures have also had a profound impact on the theoretical understanding of language and machine learning.

Research on these architectures has provided insights into the nature of language processing in the human brain and learning in general. Studies of neuron activation analyses of networks trained on NLP tasks have helped to identify striking similarities (and differences) with neural representations of languages in the human brain.

And we celebrate the progress made with deep neural networks in NLP, the community remains aware of the existing limitations and the ethical and societal challenges that come with using powerful machine learning systems.

With the increase in the capacity to train and implement these advanced models, there is a collective responsibility to ensure their responsible use and benefit for society as a whole, a mission that requires a collaborative and multidisciplinary approach, uniting technology, science, humanities and politics.

As we move forward, research remains focused not only on enhancing the ability of language models to process and generate text, but also on finding ways to make them contextually aware, ethically responsible, and able to interact harmoniously with humans.

The inclusion of more world knowledge, causal logic, and soft skills in NLP will be essential to developing AI that can effectively be a partner in people's everyday lives.

As such, future research may involve creating hybrid models that combine the statistical approaches of deep neural networks with symbolic and logical models, in the hope of overcoming persistent challenges, such as the lack of generalization beyond the training data and the difficulty of explaining model decisions and behaviors.

4   Conclusion.

This book presented an immersion in the fundamentals of prompt engineering, exploring concepts, techniques, and applications that are essential for anyone who wishes to understand and work in the field of artificial intelligence.

Throughout the chapters, we unravel the mysteries behind creating effective prompts, identify the core elements that structure these interactions, and trace the historical evolution that culminated in the powerful AI tools we know today, such as Transformers and Long Short-Term Memory (LSTMs).

We also highlight the importance of understanding the risks associated with poorly structured prompts and how well-designed prompt engineering can generate optimized results, aligned with the specific objectives of those who use them.

Along the way, it became evident that the role of the prompt transcends a simple technical instruction: it is a bridge between human intent and machine response, determining the effectiveness of solutions and the quality of interactions with AI.

This journey, however, is not only technical. It leads us to reflect on the social, ethical, and philosophical impact of this new era. Prompt engineering is not just about shaping the behavior of machines, but also about shaping how we humans communicate with these intelligences.

The power of AI systems to influence behavior requires accountability. The ability to personalize, optimize, and adjust the language that guides these technologies places in the hands of humanity the opportunity—and the duty—to ensure that these interactions are guided by ethical and humanistic values.

As we move forward in the development of AI, we will face divergent paths: we may choose to build technologies that amplify inequalities, or we may choose to develop inclusive and just solutions.

The role of humanity will be decisive in defining these directions. AI can be a tool for progress or a divisive force, depending on how it is shaped. The prompt, in this context, is more than a command; It represents our intention and our vision for the future.

What values will guide the evolution of AI? What society do we wish to build alongside these thinking machines? This book closes with the provocation that the fate of this technology is not in the hands of machines, but rather in our ability to direct it. The future of AI is, above all, the future of humanity.

This book is just one step in an essential journey in the field of artificial intelligence. This volume is part of a larger collection, "Artificial Intelligence: The Power of Data," with 49 volumes that explore, in depth, different aspects of AI and data science.

The other volumes address equally crucial topics, such as the integration of AI systems, predictive analytics, and the use of advanced algorithms for decision-making.

By purchasing and reading the other books in the collection, available on Amazon, you will have a holistic and deep view that will allow you not only to optimize data governance, but also to enhance the impact of artificial intelligence on your operations.

5   References.

BISHOP, C. (2006). Pattern Recognition and Machine Learning. Springer.

CHOLLET, F. (2021). Deep Learning with Python. Manning Publications.

DOMINGOS, P. (2015). The Master Algorithm: How the Quest for the Ultimate Learning Machine Will Remake Our World. Basic Books.

DUDA, R.; HART, P.; STORK, D. (2006). Pattern Classification. Wiley.

GERON, A. (2022). Hands-On Machine Learning with Scikit-Learn, Keras, and TensorFlow: Concepts, Tools, and Techniques to Build Intelligent Systems. O'Reilly Media.

GOLDBERG, Y. (2017). Neural Network Methods in Natural Language Processing. Morgan & Claypool Publishers.

KELLEHER, John D. (2019). Deep Learning. MIT Press.

JAMES, G.; WITTEN, D.; HASTIE, T.; TIBSHIRANI, R. (2021). An Introduction to Statistical Learning: With Applications in R. Springer.

JURAFSKY, D.; MARTIN, J. (2020). Speech and Language Processing: An Introduction to Natural Language Processing, Computational Linguistics, and Speech Recognition. Pearson.

KAPOOR, R.; MAHONEY, M. (2021). AI-Powered: How Prompt Engineering Transforms Data Into Knowledge. CRC Press.

LANGE, K. (2010). Optimization. Springer.

LECUN, Y.; BENGIO, Y. (2020). Advances in Neural Information Processing Systems. MIT Press.

MARR, B. (2018). Artificial Intelligence in Practice: How 50 Successful Companies Used AI and Prompt Engineering to Solve Problems. Wiley.

MITCHELL, T. (1997). Machine Learning. McGraw-Hill.

MOHAN, V. (2021). Mastering Prompt Engineering for AI Applications. Packt Publishing.

MULLER, A. C.; GUIDO, S. (2016). Introduction to Machine Learning with Python: A Guide for Data Scientists. O'Reilly Media.

MURPHY, K. (2012). Machine Learning: A Probabilistic Perspective. MIT Press.

PATTERSON, D.; HENNESSY, J. (2021). Computer Organization and Design: The Hardware/Software Interface. Morgan Kaufmann.

PINTO, M.V (2024 -1). Artificial Intelligence – Essential Guide. ISBN. 979-8322751175. Independently published. ASIN. B0D1N7TJL8.

RAGHU, M.; SCHMIDHUBER, J. (2020). AI Thinking: How Prompt Engineering Enhances Human-Computer Interaction. MIT Press.

RAJPUT, D. (2020). Artificial Intelligence and Machine Learning: Developing AI Solutions Using Prompt Engineering. BPB Publications.

RUSSELL, S.; NORVIG, P. (2020). Artificial Intelligence: A Modern Approach. Pearson.

SEN, S.; KAMEL, M. (2021). AI Design Patterns: Leveraging Prompt Engineering to Build Better AI Systems. Springer.

SMITH, B.; ERNST, A. (2021). Artificial Intelligence and the Future of Work: How Prompt Engineering Shapes Tomorrow's Jobs. Oxford University Press.

SUTTON, R.; BARTO, A. (2018). Reinforcement Learning: An Introduction. MIT Press.

TAO, Q. (2022). Artificial Intelligence Ethics and Prompt Engineering: Balancing Innovation with Responsibility. Routledge.

VANDERPLAS, J. (2016). Python Data Science Handbook: Essential Tools for Working with Data. O'Reilly Media.

ZHANG, Z.; DONG, Y. (2021). AI Systems: Foundations, Prompt Engineering, and Advanced Techniques. CRC Press.

6   Discover the Complete Collection "Artificial Intelligence and the Power of Data" – An Invitation to Transform Your Career and Knowledge.

The "Artificial Intelligence and the Power of Data" Collection was created for those who want not only to understand Artificial Intelligence (AI), but also to apply it strategically and practically.

In a series of carefully crafted volumes, I unravel complex concepts in a clear and accessible manner, ensuring the reader has a thorough understanding of AI and its impact on modern societies.

No matter what level of familiarity with the topic is, this collection turns the difficult into didactic, the theoretical into the applicable, and the technical into something powerful for your career.

6.1   Why buy this collection?

We are living through an unprecedented technological revolution, where AI is the driving force in areas such as medicine, finance, education, government, and entertainment.

The collection "Artificial Intelligence and the Power of Data" dives deep into all these sectors, with practical examples and reflections that go far beyond traditional concepts.

You'll find both the technical expertise and the ethical and social implications of AI encouraging you to see this technology not just as a tool, but as a true agent of transformation.

Each volume is a fundamental piece of this innovative puzzle: from machine learning to data governance and from ethics to practical application.

With the guidance of an experienced author who combines academic research with years of hands-on practice, this collection is more than a set of books — it's an indispensable guide for anyone looking to navigate and excel in this burgeoning field.

6.2   Target Audience of this Collection?

This collection is for everyone who wants to play a prominent role in the age of AI:

- ✓ Tech Professionals: Receive deep technical insights to expand their skills.

- ✓ Students and the Curious: have access to clear explanations that facilitate the understanding of the complex universe of AI.

- ✓ Managers, business leaders, and policymakers will also benefit from the strategic vision on AI, which is essential for making well-informed decisions.

- ✓ Professionals in Career Transition: Professionals in career transition or interested in specializing in AI will find here complete material to build their learning trajectory.

6.3   Much More Than Technique — A Complete Transformation.

This collection is not just a series of technical books; It is a tool for intellectual and professional growth.

With it, you go far beyond theory: each volume invites you to a deep reflection on the future of humanity in a world where machines and algorithms are increasingly present.

This is your invitation to master the knowledge that will define the future and become part of the transformation that Artificial Intelligence brings to the world.

Be a leader in your industry, master the skills the market demands, and prepare for the future with the "Artificial Intelligence and the Power of Data" collection.

This is not just a purchase; It is a decisive investment in your learning and professional development journey.

Prof. Marcão - Marcus Vinícius Pinto

M.Sc. in Information Technology.
Specialist in Artificial Intelligence, Data
Governance and Information Architecture.

7   The Books of the Collection.

7.1   Data, Information and Knowledge in the era of Artificial Intelligence.

This book essentially explores the theoretical and practical foundations of Artificial Intelligence, from data collection to its transformation into intelligence. It focuses primarily on machine learning, AI training, and neural networks.

7.2   From Data to Gold: How to Turn Information into Wisdom in the Age of AI.

This book offers critical analysis on the evolution of Artificial Intelligence, from raw data to the creation of artificial wisdom, integrating neural networks, deep learning, and knowledge modeling.

It presents practical examples in health, finance, and education, and addresses ethical and technical challenges.

7.3   Challenges and Limitations of Data in AI.

The book offers an in-depth analysis of the role of data in the development of AI exploring topics such as quality, bias, privacy, security, and scalability with practical case studies in healthcare, finance, and public safety.

7.4   Historical Data in Databases for AI: Structures, Preservation, and Purge.

This book investigates how historical data management is essential to the success of AI projects. It addresses the relevance of ISO standards to ensure quality and safety, in addition to analyzing trends and innovations in data processing.

7.5   Controlled Vocabulary for Data Dictionary: A Complete Guide.

This comprehensive guide explores the advantages and challenges of implementing controlled vocabularies in the context of AI and information science. With a detailed approach, it covers everything from the naming of data elements to the interactions between semantics and cognition.

7.6   Data Curation and Management for the Age of AI.

This book presents advanced strategies for transforming raw data into valuable insights, with a focus on meticulous curation and efficient data management. In addition to technical solutions, it addresses ethical and legal issues, empowering the reader to face the complex challenges of information.

7.7   Information Architecture.

The book addresses data management in the digital age, combining theory and practice to create efficient and scalable AI systems, with insights into modeling and ethical and legal challenges.

7.8   Fundamentals: The Essentials of Mastering Artificial Intelligence.

An essential work for anyone who wants to master the key concepts of AI, with an accessible approach and practical examples. The book explores innovations such as Machine Learning and Natural Language Processing, as well as ethical and legal challenges, and offers a clear view of the impact of AI on various industries.

7.9   LLMS - Large-Scale Language Models.

This essential guide helps you understand the revolution of Large-Scale Language Models (LLMs) in AI.

The book explores the evolution of GPTs and the latest innovations in human-computer interaction, offering practical insights into their impact on industries such as healthcare, education, and finance.

7.10   Machine Learning: Fundamentals and Advances.

This book offers a comprehensive overview of supervised and unsupervised algorithms, deep neural networks, and federated learning. In addition to addressing issues of ethics and explainability of models.

7.11   Inside Synthetic Minds.

This book reveals how these 'synthetic minds' are redefining creativity, work, and human interactions. This work presents a detailed analysis of the challenges and opportunities provided by these technologies, exploring their profound impact on society.

7.12   The Issue of Copyright.

This book invites the reader to explore the future of creativity in a world where human-machine collaboration is a reality, addressing questions about authorship, originality, and intellectual property in the age of generative AIs.

7.13   1121 Questions and Answers: From Basic to Complex – Part 1 to 4.

Organized into four volumes, these questions serve as essential practical guides to mastering key AI concepts.

Part 1 addresses information, data, geoprocessing, the evolution of artificial intelligence, its historical milestones and basic concepts.

Part 2 delves into complex concepts such as machine learning, natural language processing, computer vision, robotics, and decision algorithms.

Part 3 addresses issues such as data privacy, work automation, and the impact of large-scale language models (LLMs).

Part 4 explores the central role of data in the age of artificial intelligence, delving into the fundamentals of AI and its applications in areas such as mental health, government, and anti-corruption.

7.14   The Definitive Glossary of Artificial Intelligence.

This glossary presents more than a thousand artificial intelligence concepts clearly explained, covering topics such as Machine Learning, Natural Language Processing, Computer Vision, and AI Ethics.

- Part 1 contemplates concepts starting with the letters A to D.
- Part 2 contemplates concepts initiated by the letters E to M.
- Part 3 contemplates concepts starting with the letters N to Z.

7.15 Prompt Engineering - Volumes 1 to 6.

This collection covers all the fundamentals of prompt engineering, providing a complete foundation for professional development.

With a rich variety of prompts for areas such as leadership, digital marketing, and information technology, it offers practical examples to improve clarity, decision-making, and gain valuable insights.

The volumes cover the following subjects:

- Volume 1: Fundamentals. Structuring Concepts and History of Prompt Engineering.
- Volume 2: Tools and Technologies, State and Context Management, and Ethics and Security.
- Volume 3: Language Models, Tokenization, and Training Methods.
- Volume 4: How to Ask Right Questions.
- Volume 5: Case Studies and Errors.
- Volume 6: The Best Prompts.

7.16 Guide to Being a Prompt Engineer – Volumes 1 and 2.

The collection explores the advanced fundamentals and skills required to be a successful prompt engineer, highlighting the benefits, risks, and the critical role this role plays in the development of artificial intelligence.

Volume 1 covers crafting effective prompts, while Volume 2 is a guide to understanding and applying the fundamentals of Prompt Engineering.

7.17   Data Governance with AI – Volumes 1 to 3.

Find out how to implement effective data governance with this comprehensive collection. Offering practical guidance, this collection covers everything from data architecture and organization to protection and quality assurance, providing a complete view to transform data into strategic assets.

Volume 1 addresses practices and regulations. Volume 2 explores in depth the processes, techniques, and best practices for conducting effective audits on data models. Volume 3 is your definitive guide to deploying data governance with AI.

7.18   Algorithm Governance.

This book looks at the impact of algorithms on society, exploring their foundations and addressing ethical and regulatory issues. It addresses transparency, accountability, and bias, with practical solutions for auditing and monitoring algorithms in sectors such as finance, health, and education.

7.19   From IT Professional to AI Expert: The Ultimate Guide to a Successful Career Transition.

For Information Technology professionals, the transition to AI represents a unique opportunity to enhance skills and contribute to the development of innovative solutions that shape the future.

In this book, we investigate the reasons for making this transition, the essential skills, the best learning path, and the prospects for the future of the IT job market.

7.20   Intelligent Leadership with AI: Transform Your Team and Drive Results.

This book reveals how artificial intelligence can revolutionize team management and maximize organizational performance.

By combining traditional leadership techniques with AI-powered insights, such as predictive analytics-based leadership, you'll learn how to optimize processes, make more strategic decisions, and create more efficient and engaged teams.

7.21   Impacts and Transformations: Complete Collection.

This collection offers a comprehensive and multifaceted analysis of the transformations brought about by Artificial Intelligence in contemporary society.

- Volume 1: Challenges and Solutions in the Detection of Texts Generated by Artificial Intelligence.

- Volume 2: The Age of Filter Bubbles. Artificial Intelligence and the Illusion of Freedom.
- Volume 3: Content Creation with AI - How to Do It?
- Volume 4: The Singularity Is Closer Than You Think.
- Volume 5: Human Stupidity versus Artificial Intelligence.
- Volume 6: The Age of Stupidity! A Cult of Stupidity?
- Volume 7: Autonomy in Motion: The Intelligent Vehicle Revolution.
- Volume 8: Poiesis and Creativity with AI.
- Volume 9: Perfect Duo: AI + Automation.
- Volume 10: Who Holds the Power of Data?

7.22   Big Data with AI: Complete Collection.

The collection covers everything from the technological fundamentals and architecture of Big Data to the administration and glossary of essential technical terms.

The collection also discusses the future of humanity's relationship with the enormous volume of data generated in the databases of training in Big Data structuring.

- Volume 1: Fundamentals.
- Volume 2: Architecture.
- Volume 3: Implementation.
- Volume 4: Administration.
- Volume 5: Essential Themes and Definitions.
- Volume 6: Data Warehouse, Big Data, and AI.

8 About the Author.

I'm Marcus Pinto, better known as Prof. Marcão, a specialist in information technology, information architecture and artificial intelligence.

With more than four decades of dedicated work and research, I have built a solid and recognized trajectory, always focused on making technical knowledge accessible and applicable to all those who seek to understand and stand out in this transformative field.

My experience spans strategic consulting, education and authorship, as well as an extensive performance as an information architecture analyst.

This experience enables me to offer innovative solutions adapted to the constantly evolving needs of the technological market, anticipating trends and creating bridges between technical knowledge and practical impact.

Over the years, I have developed comprehensive and in-depth expertise in data, artificial intelligence, and information governance – areas that have become essential for building robust and secure systems capable of handling the vast volume of data that shapes today's world.

My book collection, available on Amazon, reflects this expertise, addressing topics such as Data Governance, Big Data, and Artificial Intelligence with a clear focus on practical applications and strategic vision.

Author of more than 150 books, I investigate the impact of artificial intelligence in multiple spheres, exploring everything from its technical bases to the ethical issues that become increasingly urgent with the adoption of this technology on a large scale.

In my lectures and mentorships, I share not only the value of AI, but also the challenges and responsibilities that come with its implementation – elements that I consider essential for ethical and conscious adoption.

I believe that technological evolution is an inevitable path. My books are a proposed guide on this path, offering deep and accessible insights for those who want not only to understand, but to master the technologies of the future.

With a focus on education and human development, I invite you to join me on this transformative journey, exploring the possibilities and challenges that this digital age has in store for us.

9   How to Contact Prof. Marcão.

9.1   For lectures, training and business mentoring.

marcao.tecno@gmail.com

9.2   Prof. Marcão, on Linkedin.

https://bit.ly/linkedin_profmarcao

www.ingramcontent.com/pod-product-compliance
Lightning Source LLC
LaVergne TN
LVHW051608050326
832903LV00033B/4403